Samuel French Acting Edition

From Five to Five-Thirty

A Comedy in One Act

by Philip Johnson

SAMUELFRENCH.COM   SAMUELFRENCH.CO.UK

Copyright © 1945 by Samuel French Ltd.
All Rights Reserved

FROM FIVE TO FIVE-THIRTY is fully protected under the copyright laws of the United States of America, the British Commonwealth, including Canada, and all other countries of the Copyright Union. All rights, including professional and amateur stage productions, recitation, lecturing, public reading, motion picture, radio broadcasting, television and the rights of translation into foreign languages are strictly reserved.

ISBN 978-0-573-69847-7

www.SamuelFrench.com
www.SamuelFrench.co.uk

For Production Enquiries

United States and Canada
Info@SamuelFrench.com
1-866-598-8449

United Kingdom and Europe
Plays@SamuelFrench.co.uk
020-7255-4302

Each title is subject to availability from Samuel French, depending upon country of performance. Please be aware that *FROM FIVE TO FIVE-THIRTY* may not be licensed by Samuel French in your territory. Professional and amateur producers should contact the nearest Samuel French office or licensing partner to verify availability.

CAUTION: Professional and amateur producers are hereby warned that *FROM FIVE TO FIVE-THIRTY* is subject to a licensing fee. Publication of this play(s) does not imply availability for performance. Both amateurs and professionals considering a production are strongly advised to apply to Samuel French before starting rehearsals, advertising, or booking a theatre. A licensing fee must be paid whether the title(s) is presented for charity or gain and whether or not admission is charged. Professional/Stock licensing fees are quoted upon application to Samuel French.

No one shall make any changes in this title(s) for the purpose of production. No part of this book may be reproduced, stored in a retrieval system, or transmitted in any form, by any means, now known or yet to be invented, including mechanical, electronic, photocopying, recording, videotaping, or otherwise, without the prior written permission of the publisher. No one shall upload this title(s), or part of this title(s), to any social media websites.

For all enquiries regarding motion picture, television, and other media rights, please contact Samuel French.

MUSIC USE NOTE

Licensees are solely responsible for obtaining formal written permission from copyright owners to use copyrighted music in the performance of this play and are strongly cautioned to do so. If no such permission is obtained by the licensee, then the licensee must use only original music that the licensee owns and controls. Licensees are solely responsible and liable for all music clearances and shall indemnify the copyright owners of the play(s) and their licensing agent, Samuel French, against any costs, expenses, losses and liabilities arising from the use of music by licensees. Please contact the appropriate music licensing authority in your territory for the rights to any incidental music.

IMPORTANT BILLING AND CREDIT REQUIREMENTS

If you have obtained performance rights to this title, please refer to your licensing agreement for important billing and credit requirements.

CHARACTERS

Mrs. Boxer.
Edith.
Alice.
Gertie.
Mrs. Treetops.

The play happens in the sitting-room of Mrs. Treetops' little semi-detached villa, on the afternoon of a day in summer.

N.B.—All stage directions are given from the point of view of the audience.

FROM FIVE TO FIVE-THIRTY

The SCENE *is the sitting-room of a small semi-detached house in a suburb of a manufacturing town.*

The one window is C. *back; the door, giving admittance to the diminutive hall, is down* L. *; the fireplace is in the middle of the* R. *wall. The furniture, consisting mainly of a plush-upholstered " suite," is both uninspired and uninspiring.* C., *placed at a slight angle, is a settee, and behind this is a small round table upon which is a vase of expensive-looking flowers. A larger table is set against the* L. *wall, above the door, and upon this an embroidered table-runner and another vase of flowers. To back and* R. *of this table are plush-upholstered stiff-backed chairs. Below the door is a wickerwork armchair.* C.R., *slightly more down stage than the settee, is another member of the " suite " : an easy chair. Against the back wall, to* R. *of the window, is a sideboard, and upon this are various vases, framed photographs, a cruet, a dish of apples, and another bowl of flowers. In front of the window is a very small, flimsy-looking table, supporting a large china pot in which some kind of plant copes with life. To* L. *of the window is a cabinet, and upon this another vase of flowers. The window is like a few million other suburban windows: as though to conceal unspeakable goings-on from the outside world, it is discreetly veiled with cream-coloured net. Of this prying outside world itself, little can be seen save a hazy outline of houses on the other side of the road. Above the fireplace, which is masked by a hand-painted fire-screen, is a chair upholstered with some sort of bead-work ; in front of the fireplace is a fancy pouffe ; below the fireplace, against the wall, is a small writing-table and chair. Upon the settee, the easy chair and the wicker-work chair are gaily-*

coloured cushions. Upon the mantelpiece is a clock and an assortment of little vases and knick-knacks. There are, however, no pictures on the walls. Other articles of furniture, provided that they contribute to the general scheme, may be added at the discretion of the producer.

When the CURTAIN *rises, it is the late afternoon of a day in summer, and a church clock outside chimes four times to sound the four quarters, then strikes the hour of five. The sole occupant of the room is a somewhat battered-looking female who rejoices in the name of* MRS. BOXER. *In the early sixties, florid-featured and inclined to be stout, she is wearing a black skirt, discoloured with age and dust and stains, and an old blouse with the sleeves rolled up and its front secured by a large gilt safety-pin. Upon her head, moored to her greying hair by several black-headed hatpins, is what was once a man's straw hat. . . . At the moment of our meeting her,* MRS. BOXER *appears to be taking it easy, for she is half-sitting, half-lying upon the settee, in her right hand a paper-backed novel. Holding this at almost arm's-length from her eyes, she is reading. Her mouth forms the words of what she is reading as the chimes complete their task.*

MRS. BOXER (*silently reading—we give the words of what she reads in order that her mouth may form them*). " With a careless gesture, Sir Wilfred flicked the ash from 'is costly cigar. Then, with a 'orrible leer that made poor Rosemary's blood run cold, 'e said, ' Come, my pretty one, let us stroll a little further into the wood, and I will tell you of the grand ball at the Castle last night, and snatch a kiss, perchance, from those cherry-ripe lips of yours.' At those bold words, Rosemary felt 'erself blushing from 'ead to foot. ' Indeed, Sir, I must not, for dear Grannie will be wondering where I am.' "

(*The hour strike finishes.*)

(*She breaks into audible speech.*) " ' Do not trifle with

me, girl,' 'e snarled. ' See, 'ere is a bright 'alf-crown for your missionary-box. Come, now, a kiss ! ' "

(*The front-door bell rings.*)

" ' No, no,' she faltered. ' I implore you, Sir, to stand aside and let me pass.' ' Never,' 'e cried. Then, bending over 'er, 'is 'ot breath fanning 'er face, 'e 'issed into 'er ear 'is ghastly threat : ' One kiss, now, this instant, you little fool, or I strangle you with the strings of your sun-bonnet, and fling your body to me pack of 'ounds.' "

(*At this point, the front-door bell rings again, more violently than before.*)

Oh, shut up, you !

(*Nevertheless, she rises, stuffs the novel behind a cushion, and starts unhurriedly for the door. Pausing there for a moment, she raises both hands to her hat, gives it a vicious jerk which tilts it at another and slightly aggressive angle, then opens the door and sails out. The slam of the front-door is heard, followed by the somewhat shrill sound of* MRS. PORTEOUS (EDITH) *speaking in querulous tones.*)

EDITH (*off stage*). I really cannot think, Mrs. Boxer, why it should take you so long to open a door. (*Entering.*) If there's one thing I dislike, it is being kept standing on a doorstep. I must have been there five minutes.

(EDITH *is forty, but thanks to a permanently soured expression, looks older. She is of medium height and build, with rather sharp features and lips. Everything about her, the dark, severely-cut costume, the black suède gloves, the " sensible " shoes, seem to be tight and strained. Even her hat, which only just misses being a toque, has a strained and compressed look about it. She is carrying a very plain handbag and a long-handled umbrella.*)

MRS. BOXER (*following her in—in a quite unapologetic tone*). Well, if you must know, Mrs. Porteous, I didn't know whether it was the front-door bell, or a noise in me 'ead. Something chronic they've been to-day, the noises in me 'ead. I feel all no-'ow.

EDITH (*who has gone behind the settee to* R. *of it—placing her handbag on the* R. *arm of the settee and leaning her umbrella against the* R. *corner of it*). Kindly tell Mother I'm here.

MRS. BOXER (C.L., *and slightly up stage*). As to that I'd 'ave a job. For yer Ma ain't on the premises. She's gone to the pictures.

EDITH (*surprised—and by no means pleased*). Gone to the pictures?

MRS. BOXER (*nodding*). Set off straight after lunch. It's All-ROMANCE Week at the Odeon, and she's been every day since Monday. It takes 'er out of 'erself.

EDITH. But—but I wrote to her and told her that my two sisters and I would be calling to-day. I suppose she got my letter.

MRS. BOXER. Oh, yes, and she said she'd get 'ome early. Seeing as 'ow *you'd* be 'ere, she wouldn't wait for the comic.

EDITH (*irritably*). She should have been here now! It's most inconsiderate of her!

MRS. BOXER. I dunno. She's seventy years old. I reckon she can please 'erself, eh?

EDITH (*who has moved to behind the settee—her attention suddenly distracted by the little table*). The dust on this little table, Mrs. Boxer! I could write my name on it!

MRS. BOXER. Ah. It puts me in mind of me first place. A proper Tartar for dust, the missis was. "Katie," she'd say, " I could write me name on the pianner," she'd say. So one day I says to 'er, " I wonder you don't write something interesting, for a change." That shut 'er up, all right.

(EDITH *turns impatiently away from the table.* MRS. BOXER " *makes a face* " *towards her back, hastily re-arranging her features as* EDITH *turns towards her again.*)

And 'ow's the dear Vicar to-day?

EDITH (*curtly*). My husband is well, I thank you.

MRS. BOXER. 'Ardly looks it, does 'e ? Last time I saw 'im, 'e looked as though you could knock 'im down with a fly's eyelash ! If you ask me, a good beef-steak's what *'e* needs !

EDITH (*icily*). My husband and I, Mrs. Boxer, are strict vegetarians.

MRS. BOXER. When it comes to food, give me something what's wagged its tail.

EDITH (*her attention again distracted*). Good gracious me, where on earth did all these flowers come from ?

MRS. BOXER. Yer ma bought 'em yesterday.

EDITH (*staring at them*). But—but they must have cost Heaven knows what !

MRS. BOXER. Ah, I expect they was a bit pricey ; but only the best's good enough for yer ma, these days.

EDITH (*half under her breath*). *Monstrous!*

(*The front-door bell rings—louder.*)

And that, Mrs. Boxer, was *not* a noise in your head.

MRS. BOXER (*not stirring*). Oh, that was the front-door, all right. I wonder 'oo it can be.

EDITH (*controlling herself with an obvious effort*). It will be one of my sisters. Will you *kindly* let her in at *once* ?

MRS. BOXER (*quite leisurely—unpinning the gilt safety-pin, shifting it slightly and pinning it again*). Anything to oblige, so long as I don't 'ave to stoop or climb or stretch or lift. As the doctor says to me only the other day, " Ladies like you," 'e says, " is delicate 'ot-'ouse plants, and should be treated according."

EDITH (*losing patience*). Mrs. Boxer, *please* ! The *door* !

MRS. BOXER. Oh !—Oh, course.

(*She goes unhurriedly towards the door, pauses, raises both hands as previously to her hat, tilts it to another angle, then goes out.* EDITH *gives vent to an impatient exclamation. Going to up* R., *by the sideboard, she takes up the bowl of flowers, glares at them for a second, then puts it down again. Simultaneously, the front door is heard to slam.*)

EDITH (*muttering*). Not a penny less than ten shillings a bunch! Scandalous! (*As* ALICE *enters.*) Ah, Alice!

(MRS. PRESCOTT (ALICE) *is thirty-six. She is about the same height and build as her sister, but more fussily dressed : a floral-patterned frock, white gloves, and a wide-brimmed hat trimmed with marguerites and cornflowers. She is carrying a raffia shopping-basket in which are a few small parcels and her handbag.*)

ALICE. Edith! I'm not late, am I? (*Putting her basket on the table* L.) And I mustn't stay long, dear. I *think* the new nurse is all right, but I'm taking *no* risks.

EDITH (*coming down to* R. *of the settee*). How are the children?

ALICE (*starting to remove her gloves*). The chicks? Well, Lambkin was sick this morning, and of course I rang Dr. Willoughby. You know how abrupt he can be—all he said was, "It's the weather—cascara," and rang off. But Baby's *very* well, and what do you think he did just before I left?

EDITH. I've no idea.

ALICE. He looked straight at me, with the sweetest smile, and said, "Dum—dum—dum!" Quite obviously, it didn't *mean* anything, but it was the way he *said* it. (*She places her gloves on the table.*)

MRS. BOXER (*putting her head in at the door*). I don't know if you fancy a cupper tea. I could manage it in 'alf an 'our or so.

EDITH. No, thank you.
MRS. BOXER. Good.

(*She withdraws her head and disappears.*)

ALICE (*taking her handbag from her basket*). And, oh, you *must* see the new snaps of Baby and Lambkin. I popped them into my bag, especially to show you.

EDITH. Not just now—later. I wrote to you and Gertie, to meet me here, because, quite frankly, Alice, something has got to be done about Mother.

ALICE (*replacing her bag in the basket*). Is she upstairs?

EDITH. She is not! I wrote her that we were coming, and I arrive here to find that she has gone to the pictures.

ALICE (*moving a few paces to* C.L., *between the table and the settee*). Well, I *do* think that's thoughtless of her. Supposing she brings a germ away with her, and gives it to me, and I carry it home to the chicks.

EDITH. Mother's impossible! She's always been irresponsible, but now, at the age of seventy, she seems to have lost her head completely.

ALICE (*going to in front of the* L. *end of the settee*). But, Edith, what *can* we do?

EDITH. Talk to her—and let her see that *this* time we mean what we say!

ALICE. But, d'you think she'll listen? You know, Edith, I don't think she really likes us very much. I don't even think she likes the chicks. She was *most* unsympathetic about Lambkin's adenoids.

EDITH. She'll *have* to listen! Where would she be, if it weren't for us? She hasn't a penny in the world of her own! I'm sure I don't look for thanks, Alice, but at least she needn't shame us publicly! (*Going to* R., *by the fireplace.*)

ALICE. What?

EDITH (*by the fireplace—turning—facing* ALICE *across the room*). Yesterday morning, Arthur, if you please, was walking along High Street with two of his churchwardens. As they passed "The Market Tavern," who should come out but Mother!

ALICE (*very shocked*). No!!

EDITH. Mother! Wiping her lips on her handkerchief, just like—like any common woman!

ALICE. Oh, Edith! Oh, but that's *dreadful*! (*She sinks down upon the* L. *end of the settee.*)

EDITH. Shaken as Arthur was, he'd the presence of mind to pretend not to see her. But *that* didn't help. She marched straight up to him and said, " Hello, Arthur! You're a bit too late! I've just been having a sherry."

ALICE (*murmuring*). Good heavens!

EDITH. Arthur gave her a look and said, " Really? Aren't you feeling well? " And what d'you think Mother said?

(ALICE *shakes her head.*)

" I'm perfectly well; but if I felt half as washed-out as you look, I'd have had two more sherries! "

ALICE (*faintly*). Oh dear.

EDITH. Poor Arthur arrived home trembling. I have never *seen* him so upset, *never!* . . . *I* sat down and wrote to you and Gertie to meet me here.

(*The front-door bell rings.*)

That will be Gertie. (*She moves to in front of the easy chair.*)

ALICE. To *think* of Mother in a public-house! Supposing the Frobishers had seen her coming out, or the Wilkinsons, or the Drake-Westmacotts!

EDITH (*grimly*). They'll hear of it soon enough! Mother's determined, it seems, to make herself the talk of the town—and that's that!

ALICE (*tearfully—taking her handkerchief from her handbag*). It's too humiliating! It is, really! I feel I shall never, never lift my head again! (*Dabbing at her nose with her handkerchief.*)

EDITH. Now, Alice, put that handkerchief away. Crying won't help us.

(*The front-door is heard to slam.*)

ALICE (*still dabbing*). I'm thankful for one thing, anyway. (*Sniff.*) Lambkin and Baby are too young to realize—yet. (*Sniff, sniff.*)

(Mrs. Boxer *appears in the doorway.*)

Mrs. Boxer (*as she appears*). 'Ere's yer sister—and what d'yer think she's brought with 'er ? (*Just within the room.*) A black eye—oh, a proper beauty —you never saw such a sight !

(*She backs slightly up stage and utters a loud laugh, as* Gertie *enters.* Alice *rises, stuffing her handkerchief into her handbag.* Gertie *is thirty-eight, taller, and of a more hefty build than her sisters, and with a somewhat weather-beaten complexion. Her dress consists of a tweed skirt, brogue shoes, an open-neck shirt-blouse, and a knitted cardigan. She is not wearing a hat, and has a black eye.*)

Edith (*exclaiming as she enters*). Why, Gertie, whatever——

Gertie. It's all right ! Don't fuss ! I got it in the hockey-match, yesterday, against Saint Ursula's. It's nothing.

Mrs. Boxer. All this 'ere 'ockeying's beyond me. In my young days, if a girl could strum the pianner, and do a tambourine-dance, she was 'appy. But now, blimey ! They act like they're training for a bull-fight.

Edith. Mrs. Boxer, that is quite enough.

Mrs. Boxer. You're right, it is. (*To* Gertie.) And maybe when you've blacked yer other eye, and knocked yer front teeth out, it'll be enough for you, too.

(*She goes out.*)

Gertie. Really, that woman ! Why Mother should harbour her about the house is beyond me !

Edith. Practically everything that Mother does these days is beyond me ! (*She sits in the easy chair.*)

Alice (*explosively*). Gertie, she's behaving disgracefully, and *something* has got to be *done* ! (*She sits again on the settee.*)

Edith. And we're here to-day to tell her so !

* *

GERTIE. Well, of course, what *I* want to know is this! where's she getting the money from?

EDITH. I don't begrudge the thirty shillings a week we each allow her, but four pounds ten a week seems a lot for an old lady whose wants should only be very simple.

GERTIE. Apparently, that's just what they're not.

(*A very short pause. They sense some meaning behind her words, and look at her, questioningly.*)

It may interest both of you to know that the day before yesterday, Mother went into Dobson's and ordered four new hats, a costume, two afternoon frocks, and an evening-dress, a dozen pairs of stockings, and nine pairs of shoes.

ALICE }
EDITH } (*together, staring at her, aghast*). *What?*

GERTIE. She then ran gaily amok in the music department, and played on all the grand pianos, one after another!

ALICE (*almost plaintively*). Gertie, she didn't buy a grand piano?

GERTIE. She said she'd think it over, and send them a postcard.

(*There is a stricken silence.* ALICE, *words failing her, shakes her head helplessly. Then, as though unable to sit still,* EDITH *suddenly springs to her feet.*)

EDITH (*in an outburst*). It's wicked! Downright wicked! (*She strides to up* R., *then swings round.*) Buying a lot of clothes she can't possibly want! Spending money like water!

ALICE (*in a high-pitched voice*). But she hasn't got it to spend! She must have persuaded Dobson's to let her open an account!

EDITH (*seething—back to by the* R. *end of the settee*). I dare say! And given Arthur's name as a reference! Oh, it's—it's——

ALICE. And Henry's as well, you can depend!

EDITH. Running up bills all over the place! Look at these flowers! I, at the Vicarage, if you please, have to be content with a vase or two of sweet-peas, and a bowl of Dorothy Perkins in the hall!

ALICE. But—she'll never be able to pay for the things!

EDITH. No! In the end, either your Henry and my Arthur will have to do that to keep her out of the County Court, or she'll have the bailiffs in the house.

GERTIE (*going to by the* L. *arm of the settee*). She'd enjoy that. She'd probably put on her evening-dress, and play cards with them in the kitchen.

ALICE (*her feelings overcoming her again—fumbling in her bag and producing her handkerchief*). Oh!

EDITH. Of course, there's always been a rakish streak in Mother—Bohemian, as they call it! Everything slap-dash and hugger-mugger, with meals at any hour, and supper things never washed up till next morning, and telling bare-faced lies to the tradespeople when she couldn't pay the bills, and buying fancy tea-gowns when she hadn't a decent pair of shoes to her feet—oh, she's hopeless—hopeless, and always was! (*She turns and sits down heavily in the easy chair.*)

GERTIE (*sitting on the* L. *arm of the settee*). I suspect her childhood was all wrong. Didn't play the right sort of games. It's fatal.

ALICE (*sniffing and dabbing at her nose*). Why can't she be like my Henry's mother, who's been bed-ridden for ten years, and calls the chicks her two little sunbeams?

GERTIE. The question is : what are we going to do about her ? We can't go on like this !

EDITH. Don't worry ; we're not going to !

(ALICE *stuffs her handkerchief back into her bag. A barely perceptible pause. Then* EDITH *rises—with a great air of resolution and determination.*)

Mother's leaving the town ! She's going away from here—and what's more, she's never coming back !

ALICE (*staring at her*). Has she said so ?

EDITH. She doesn't know it, yet. All the same, she's going—to a lovely house in the country, miles away, called Sunset House. (*She takes a brochure from her bag and tosses it on to the settee, beside* ALICE.) You can read all about it, there. (*She goes towards down* L.)

(ALICE *picks up the brochure and looks at the cover.*)

GERTIE (*going to behind the settee*). Is it a sort of hotel, Edith ?

ALICE (*reading from the cover of the brochure*). " Sunset House, where, midst beautiful surroundings, with central heating, and liberal table, old age may spend and end its days in tranquillity and peace. Lovingly tended Garden of Sleep quite near at hand, though not within sight of the house."

EDITH. It's a Home for elderly gentlewomen, and we're very, very lucky indeed to have heard of it.

ALICE (*turning the pages of the brochure*). Look, here's a bit of poetry : " When the sun of your life starts to sink to the West, come to the Sunset Home of Rest.—Terms : Four Guineas a week."

GERTIE (*behind the settee—reading over* ALICE'S *shoulder*). And here's a testimonial : " The thought that my dear mother-in-law is now with you at Sunset House has lifted a great load from my mind." (*As* ALICE *turns a page*.) What's that photograph ?— that sort of queer bundle ?

ALICE (*reading*). " Our oldest inhabitant, aged ninety-two, suns herself happily upon the lawn." (*Holding the brochure very near to her eyes*.) Look ! You can just see her nose peeping out through her shawls ! Isn't it *sweet* ?

EDITH. Sunset House is the perfect answer to our problem. With Mother safely there, we shall breathe freely for the first time for years—I know I shall.

ALICE (*lowering the brochure to her lap*). But, Edith, is it—is it a sort of institution ? I wouldn't like to think of the chicks' grandmother being in a place like that—I wouldn't, really.

EDITH. Don't be silly ! How can it be when they charge four guineas a week ?

ALICE (*closing the brochure—placing it beside her on the settee*). She won't go. You know what Mother is.

EDITH (*firmly*). Either she goes to Sunset House, or we stop her allowance—instantly. And let her see that this time we mean it. We've paid the piper quite long enough, I fancy : it's about time that we called the tune !

ALICE (*rising suddenly—weakly*). I hate upsets like this. She'll make a scene, Edith, you know she will.

EDITH. Let her ! (*Impatiently.*) For heaven's sake, Alice, don't be so weak ! So long as Mother's in this town, you and Gertie and I are on the edge of a volcano. We never know what she may be up to next, to shame us—and it's got to stop.

ALICE (*going towards down* L.). Yes, I know . . . but it would be so much nicer if—well—if she'd go to this place of her own accord. . . . I mean, if we *could* persuade her . . . we'd feel so much happier about it all—later—than if we'd forced her into it—wouldn't we ?

EDITH. I'm perfectly willing to *try* persuasion, but if that fails——

GERTIE. And it will, if I know Mother.

ALICE (*down* L.—*trying to soothe her conscience*). Of course there's always the chance that she may be quite happy there . . . in time, I mean.

EDITH. After all, how do you prefer to think of Mother ? Sunning herself on the lawn at Sunset House, or reeling out of public-houses with her hat over one eye ?

ALICE (*sitting on the chair by the writing-table*). Oh, Edith, you didn't say she was reeling !

EDITH (*evading the direct answer*). In a year from

now, at the rate she's going, she'll probably be falling down and lying in the gutter!

GERTIE. Hush! I thought I heard—— (*She starts to hurry towards the window but halts as the front door is heard to slam.*) She's here! It's Mother.

ALICE (*agitatedly*). Oh dear! Edith—don't forget—we try persuasion first——

EDITH. Ssssh!

MRS. TREETOPS' VOICE (*off stage*). Katie! Katie! Where are you?

(*The door-handle rattles, as though someone not having the perfectly free use of their hands is trying to turn it. Then the door bursts open, and* MRS. TREETOPS *stands revealed in the doorway. She is, as has already been impressed upon us, seventy years old, though one would hardly guess it from her appearance. She is, in fact, one of those people who from the age of fifty or so change but little in looks or in spirit. An increasing mellowness there may be; but the more accepted paraphernalia of advancing years, the wrinkled skin, the sagging muscles, the stooping figure, the quavering voice, these signs and tokens somehow seem to pass them by.* MRS. TREETOPS *is wearing a quite attractive dress, and a hat which, without being stupidly "girlish," still suggests a certain youthfulness. And she is laden, utterly laden, with sheaves and bunches of flowers. Both arms, in fact, are quite full.*)

(*As she enters.*) Here I am, at last, girls, here I am! Have you been waiting long? (*Without waiting for a reply, she calls over her shoulder.*) Katie! Katie! (*Dropping her voice to normal.*) Where on earth is the woman? (*Calling again—much louder.*) Katie!

MRS. BOXER'S VOICE (*off stage—some distance away*). I'm 'ere, Missis! What d'yer want?

MRS. TREETOPS (*calling*). I've bought some more flowers! Bring bowls and vases and jugs and things!

MRS. BOXER'S VOICE (*as before*). Righto!

(*During this, the three, momentarily taken aback by this new evidence of their mother's extravagance, stare aghast.* EDITH *is standing in front of the* R. *end of the settee;* GERTIE *is just above the fireplace;* ALICE, *who has risen at her mother's entrance, is still down* R.)

GERTIE. *Mother!*

MRS. TREETOPS. Just a minute, dear, while I—— (*She leans over the table* L., *and opens her arms. The flowers cascade to the table in a mass.*) There!

EDITH (*with acid sarcasm*). You've been buying a few flowers, I see.

MRS. TREETOPS. Aren't they lovely ? Of course, I can't have any more in *this* room. These will have to go up in my bedroom. (*With a gay little laugh.*) I shall feel like a film star, or a king's plaything, shan't I ?

EDITH (*with heavy disapproval*). Flowers in a bedroom are most unhealthy.

MRS. TREETOPS. And how are you, Edith ? You and Arthur still munching rabbit-food ?

EDITH (*stiffly*). We adhere to our vegetarian principles, Mother, if that's what you mean.

MRS. TREETOPS. Well, don't try to convert me, that's all. The last time I had a meal at your house, my tummy rumbled like a runaway lorry for hours. —Good heavens, Gertie ! What *have* you done to your eye ?

GERTIE. *I* haven't done anything. A hockey-stick did it. (*She sits very abruptly on the bead-worked chair.*)

MRS. TREETOPS (*her head on one side—studying the effect*). M'mmm ! D'you know, I believe it improves you ? A touch of what the French call *farouche*. You should always wear it.—Hullo, Alice, how are the brats ?

ALICE (*drawing herself up*). The *chicks* are quite well, thank you, Mother.

MRS. TREETOPS. Chicks ! My dear Alice, you're

not only talking like a broody hen—you're beginning to look like one. It's partly that hat, I think. Thank you, Katie! On the table, please.

(MRS. BOXER *has come in, bearing a large metal tray, upon which are several jugs and vases filled with water.*)

MRS. BOXER (*setting the tray down on the downstage end of the table*). My! Ain't they choice, eh? Almost as good as artificial!

MRS. TREETOPS (*by the table*). Lovely! See, we'll just ram them in anyhow. I'll arrange them later. (*They proceed to thrust the flowers haphazard into the jugs and vases.*) There! . . . That's it. . . . You can leave them here, Katie, and then I can look at them now and then while I'm talking to the girls (*with a somewhat wry glance towards* EDITH), or they're talking to me.

MRS. BOXER. That's right! 'Ave a nice talk. Let yer back 'air down and loosen your stays. So long.

(*She goes out, closing the door behind her.*)

GERTIE (*the moment the door is closed—springing to her feet*). Really, Mother, the way you allow that dreadful woman to talk and go on, it's—it's scandalous!

MRS. TREETOPS (*gently*). Now, Gertie dear, it's no use trying to look indignant—not with that coloured eye. You merely look like a female pirate in a pet. (*She giggles.*)

(GERTIE, *about to retort, restrains herself and goes up to by the window.*)

ALICE. Gertie's quite right to be indignant. You allow the woman to talk as though she were a friend!

MRS. TREETOPS. Well, so she is. (*Going to down* L., *taking the cushion from the wicker-chair and giving it a little shake.*) She makes me laugh—and anyone who makes me laugh is a friend.

EDITH. Friend! A woman like that, who's nothing but a—a——

MRS. TREETOPS. Ssssh! Please, Edith! (*A little gesture with the cushion towards the flowers.*) Not in front of the roses!

EDITH. A low, vulgar creature!

MRS. TREETOPS (*lightly*). Oh, is that all? (*She replaces the cushion.*)

EDITH (*working herself up*). No, it is not! Far from it! We're here this afternoon, Mother, to put an end to things, once—and—for—all!

MRS. TREETOPS. Dear me, how sinister that sounds! An end to things! Just like three avenging angels!

EDITH. And you'll do no good this time, let me tell you, by trying to turn everything into a stupid joke!

GERTIE (*by the window*). No, indeed! Things have gone on quite long enough!

EDITH. And we're here this afternoon to tell you——

ALICE (*checking her*). Edith! (*Hurrying to her.*) Edith, don't forget what we said! (*Dropping her voice.*) Persuasion first.

(EDITH, *with an almost visible effort, controls herself, and :*)

EDITH. H'm! (*Picking up the brochure from the settee.*) This little booklet here—I should like you to glance at it, Mother, if you please.

MRS. TREETOPS (*going to her—taking it*). Why, of course. Thank you, Edith. (*She sits in an easy attitude on the* L. *end of the settee, and looks at the cover.*) "Sunset House"—what a pretty name!

ALICE (*by the* R. *arm of the settee—eagerly*), Yes, isn't it pretty?

MRS. TREETOPS (*opening the brochure*). And here's a picture of it. But what is it? Oh, I see! (*Reading.*) "Home for Elderly Gentlewomen"! How very nice.

(GERTIE *comes down to by the* L. *arm of the settee.*)

EDITH (*significantly*). I'm glad you think so, Mother.

MRS. TREETOPS. Oh, I do. And when are you thinking of going, Edith?

EDITH. *I?*

MRS. TREETOPS. And will Arthur go with you? He isn't *really* an elderly gentlewoman, is he? But perhaps they'll never notice.

ALICE. But, Mother, it isn't——

EDITH (*checking her*). Quiet!

(ALICE *sits abruptly in the easy chair.* EDITH *sits on the* R. *end of the settee, slightly sideways, to face* MRS. TREETOPS. *Speaking very deliberately.*)

It's you, Mother, who are going to Sunset House.

MRS. TREETOPS. I? Don't be silly!

EDITH (*very firmly*). We've talked it over, and we've *quite* decided.

GERTIE (*going towards down* L.). You should think yourself lucky, Mother. I'm sure I should.

ALICE (*hastily*). And it *isn't* an institution or anything nasty like that—is it, Edith?

MRS. TREETOPS (*checking* EDITH, *who is about to speak—sitting rather more upright*). Just a minute. Have you three been planning to—to put me away?

EDITH. There's no need to put it like that. The time has come to take steps, and we're taking them.

MRS. TREETOPS (*with a sudden flash of anger—tartly*). Then let me tell you at once, Edith, you're taking them in the wrong direction! Nothing on earth would induce me to go to your wretched Moonshine House. Me, indeed! Among a lot of decaying gentlewomen? No, *thank* you! (*Her anger suddenly subsiding—with a little laugh.*) Oh dear! Can you see me?

EDITH (*sternly and deliberately*). Mother, you are not going to laugh this off!

MRS. TREETOPS. But—I'm perfectly happy where I am——

EDITH (*significantly*). Possibly. But *we*, let me tell you, are *not*!

GERTIE. You've been behaving very badly, Mother—you know you have.

EDITH. Quite disgracefully! The other day—coming out of "The Market Tavern."

MRS. TREETOPS. Well, one must come out sometime.

EDITH. Poor Arthur was horrified.

MRS. TREETOPS. My dear Edith, I've been into "The Market Tavern" several times lately. It's warm and cosy and friendly, and the barmaid calls me 'dear.' It's a long, long time since anyone else called me 'dear.'

ALICE. But you'll soon make friends among the old ladies at Sunset House! Really *nice* friends, Mother!

MRS. TREETOPS. Yes, I can just picture them, with pink cotton-wool in their ears, and the Benger's Food flowing like water. (*Shaking her head.*) Oho, no! It won't do, girls! You can't get rid of the body like that.

EDITH (*controlling herself again*). Now, listen, Mother, we don't want any fuss, but you're going to Sunset House. On that we're quite determined!

GERTIE. If you'd been content to behave like any other old lady of seventy, all would have been well. (*She sits in the wicker-chair.*)

ALICE. We never know what you may be up to next to shame us; and we can't stand the strain any more.

EDITH. You don't seem to realize it, but we three have a certain position in this town. Alice here is married to the best solicitor in the place.

MRS. TREETOPS. Only the best is good enough for Alice. You can tell that by her hat.

EDITH (*ignoring this*). Gertie is games mistress at the High School, while *I* am married to the Vicar of the Parish.

MRS. TREETOPS. From the age of ten, Edith, you

were firmly determined to marry into the Church. No less than three pale young Curates packed in a hurry and fled the town before you finally got Arthur into a corner.

EDITH (*shrilly*). I did no such thing! Arthur begged and implored and beseeched me to marry him, time and again, before I said Yes! He was nearly frantic!

MRS. TREETOPS (*soothingly*). All right, Edith. There's no need to make him sound like a servant-girl in trouble.

EDITH (*springing to her feet*). Oh! You're impossible! (*Striding to down* R., *by the writing-table, then swinging round.*) You were always erratic, but now you must be going out of your mind! That's the very kindest thing that I can say of you!

MRS. TREETOPS (*quite unperturbed*). How like you, Edith dear, to think of the very kindest thing.

GERTIE. Edith's perfectly right!—Just look at all these flowers! Sheer wicked extravagance.

EDITH. And what about all those ridiculous things you bought at Dobson's the other day!

MRS. TREETOPS (*mildly*). Just a little harmless shopping. Surely——

EDITH. Harmless! What did the bill come to? (*As* MRS. TREETOPS *is silent—louder—a step towards her.*) Don't you hear me, Mother? Where is the bill? Let me see it!

(*But still no word, nor even the slightest movement, from* MRS. TREETOPS.)

ALICE. After all, Mother, *we* shall have to settle it in the end.

GERTIE (*rising—to* MRS. TREETOPS). You've nothing to gain by being stubborn, you know. (*To* EDITH.) It'll be in her writing-table.

(EDITH *turns swiftly to the writing-table, drags open the drawer, rummages determinedly among some papers, then with an* "Ah!" *snatches one forth.* MRS. TREETOPS *rises, takes a step towards* EDITH, *then halts.*)

EDITH (*glancing at the bill*). *Seventy-three pounds!!*
GERTIE. *What!*

ALICE (*rising*). Oh, *Mother!* (*Starting to hurry to* EDITH.) Let me look!

EDITH (*waving her back with one hand—staring perplexedly at the bill*). Wait a minute . . . this is a *receipted* bill!

ALICE (*to* MRS. TREETOPS—*incredulously*). D'you mean—you've actually *paid* for the things?

(MRS. TREETOPS *is about to deliver a heated retort to this, but checks herself. Instead, she marches very determinedly to* EDITH, *snatches the bill from her, thrusts it into the drawer, and slams the drawer to.*)

MRS. TREETOPS. If you can behave like a female thug on lettuce and lentils, Edith, God knows what you'd be like after good beef-steak! (*She turns and goes to* C.R., *by the fireplace.*)

GERTIE (*during* MRS. TREETOPS' *move*). But, Mother, you can't—I mean, how—where did the money come from? You *can't* have saved all that!

EDITH. She never saved a penny in her life, and well you know it! (*Going to just below* MRS. TREETOPS, *and slightly to* L. *of her—her back to the audience.*) There's something fishy about this! I insist that you tell us at once where you got all this money to squander!

(MRS. TREETOPS' *lips curve to a little smile. She may be contemplating a reply, but it is never spoken, for :*)

ALICE (*suddenly—excitedly*). She doesn't have to tell me! I *knew* there was something different about this room! (*Hurrying to up* C.—*pointing to the wall over the fireplace.*) Look! The picture's gone! Shes' sold the picture!

(EDITH *and* GERTIE, *thus prompted, stare at the pictureless wall.*)

MRS. TREETOPS (*still with the little smile*). Well, now, I do call that clever of our little broody hen.

She's right. I've sold the picture. Vernon took it soon after we were married, in part payment of a debt—and it was mine to do as I liked with.

EDITH. But it was an awful thing! So dirty and dark, you could hardly tell what it was about.

MRS. TREETOPS (*lightly*). The man seemed pleased enough with it. He said it would clean up beautifully.

GERTIE But—he couldn't have given you seventy-odd pounds. (*To* EDITH.) It wasn't worth as many shillings.

MRS. TREETOPS. As a matter of fact, he gave me rather more . . . fifteen thousand pounds.

(*She says this quite simply, with no dramatic emphasis whatever. Nevertheless, the effect upon the three is devastating. For a moment, indeed, they are completely bereft of speech and movement, and the chaos into which their minds have so unceremoniously been hurled can scarcely be termed thought. They don't even gasp: they just stare, that's all. Needless to say, it is* EDITH *who first recovers her voice—or some semblance of it.*)

EDITH. Mother . . . will you . . . say that again?

MRS. TREETOPS. Why, certainly. I love saying it. Fifteen thousand pounds, fifteen thousand pounds, fifteen thousand pounds.

(*Another very short pause. The three still stare at her. Then:*)

GERTIE (*suddenly—almost violently*). It isn't true! It couldn't be! (*To* MRS. TREETOPS.) This is one of your so-called jokes, isn't it?

(*For answer,* MRS. TREETOPS *goes briskly to the sideboard, takes a folded newspaper which is lying there, then goes to* EDITH *and thrusts it into her hand.*)

MRS. TREETOPS (*pointing to a paragraph*). That bit, there. Read it, Edith dear, read it.

EDITH (*looking at* MRS. TREETOPS, *then at the paper*

—*reading*). " Sensational Art Discovery. Valuable painting in Suburban Villa." (*From this point she reads to herself, her eyes skimming the lines, her lips moving rapidly, until she comes to the three magical words.*) " Fifteen thousand pounds." It's *true* !— *Alice !*—*Gertie !*—it's *true* !

GERTIE (*hurrying to* EDITH). Here, let me see——

(*But she is too late, for* ALICE *gets there first and snatches the paper.*)

ALICE (*reading breathlessly*). " Superb landscape by Giovanni Minetti . . . thought to have been lost . . . windfall for widow . . . fifteen thou——*"* (*She breaks off—the hand holding the paper falling limply to her side—shaking her head, dazedly.*) It's no use. . . . I know this isn't really happening . . . there'll be a knock at the door in a minute—the morning tea— and I shall wake up.

MRS. TREETOPS (*going a little up stage*). And there beside you, will be a picture no artist could paint— Henry !

(GERTIE *takes the paper from* ALICE, *and starts to move slowly towards down* R., *reading, her head slightly on one side as she focuses the print with her sound eye.* EDITH, *who has now recovered somewhat, takes* ALICE *by the arm, and leads her to the settee.*)

EDITH. Sit down, Alice.

(*Obediently, though still dazedly,* ALICE *sits. There is another very short pause.* GERTIE, *down* R., *her back to the others, is reading.* EDITH *moves a few paces towards* L., *busily adjusting herself to the new situation.* MRS. TREETOPS, *up* R.C., *looks with twinkling eyes at each one in turn, as though vastly amused at her own private thoughts.*)

GERTIE (*tossing the paper on to the writing-table— excitedly*). But, Mother—Mother, when—I mean, how—did it happen ?

Mrs. Treetops. Well, if you must know, it was really through my friend, Mr. Smithers, from the antique-shop.

Edith. That awful man! Drinks like a fish, and beats his wife, they say, with a toasting-fork!

Mrs. Treetops. I expect it serves her right; and, anyway, it's a picturesque toasting-fork—centuries old—he showed it to me once.

Edith. And you make a friend of a man like that! Good heavens!

Mrs. Treetops. Certainly, I do. He comes round here quite often in the evenings, and he's taught Katie and me to play a lovely game called Crown and Anchor.

Gertie (*before* Edith *can speak*). What's he got to do with the picture?

Mrs. Treetops. Well, he happened to notice it one night, and, after he'd put on his spectacles and looked at it closer, he said, "Mrs. T., unless I'm very much mistaken, you've got something there. If that isn't an honest-to-God genuine Minetti, then my name isn't Smithers!"

Edith. Well?

Mrs. Treetops. And, anyway, he wrote to a gentleman in London about it, and the gentleman came down and looked at it; and he wrote to another gentleman, and *he* came, too; and then three gentlemen came in a Rolls-Royce car—in fact, in less than a week, no less than nine strange gentlemen called at this house. And then they decided it was a Minetti picture, all right, and what would I take for it? Before I could answer at all, dear Mr. Smithers chipped in. "Mrs. Treetops may be tempted by fifteen thousand pounds," he said. I nearly fainted. "Yes, we are willing to pay that if we can take it away with us," they said. I just had strength enough to say, "Yes, take it." (*She says the last three words as if it were the last effort she could make.*)

Edith. But—fifteen thousand pounds! Just think! I can hardly grasp it.

MRS. TREETOPS (*dryly*). You don't have to, Edith. I've already done all the grasping that was needed.

EDITH. And—and you've really *got* the money?

MRS. TREETOPS (*with a nod*). You should have seen the bank manager's face when I took the cheque in. He invited me into his little room and called me " madam " seventeen times in ten minutes.

GERTIE (*staring at her*). It means that you're a wealthy woman now, Mother—*really* wealthy!

EDITH (*also staring*). It's *wonderful*! Really *wonderful*!

MRS. TREETOPS (*lightly*). Yes, isn't it? (*To* ALICE.) Alice, do, for goodness' sake, come out of that trance.

ALICE (*recovering speech*). I was just wondering— we've got an old picture in the servant's bedroom—a little boy in a velvet suit, blowing bubbles.

GERTIE. What *I* can't get over is Mother, sitting in this room for years and years, with all that money staring down at her from the wall!

MRS. TREETOPS. Ah, it makes you think, doesn't it?

EDITH. It does, indeed! (*She has achieved a swift rearrangement of her voice and expression.*) Of course—h'm!—of course, this puts *quite* a different look on things. There can be no question now of Sunset House.

MRS. TREETOPS. There never was.

EDITH (*hastily*). Well—well, there's no need to go into that now. (*She attempts a little laugh.*) Circumstances alter cases, don't they?— (*As* MRS. TREETOPS *is about to sit in the bead-work chair.*) No, no, sit in the easy chair, Mother. You'll be more comfortable.

(MRS. TREETOPS *sits in the easy-chair.*)

That's better. (*An idea striking her, she snatches up a cushion from the settee, hurries with it to* MRS. TREE- TOPS, *and stuffs it behind her back.*) *There!*

(Mrs. Treetops *immediately removes it and drops it to the floor.*)

Why, Mother——

Mrs. Treetops. Cushions are all right for old people. I'm only seventy.

(Gertie *darts to the cushion, picks it up, half-runs to the settee, and replaces it.*)

And what are you racing about for, Gertie? You're not on the hockey-field now! Sit down, and don't fuss! And you, too, Edith!

(Gertie *sits abruptly on the* L. *end of the settee.* Edith *starts to go towards the wicker-chair.*)

No, not there! On the settee!

(Edith *hesitates a second, then sits on the settee, between* Gertie *and* Alice.)

That's right. The three of you in a row!

Edith (*sensing something in* Mrs. Treetops' *tone that she does not quite like—with a little nervous laugh*). Just as though we were back at school, eh, Mother? (*The little laugh dies suddenly.*) Mother—why do you look at us like that?

Mrs. Treetops (*not speaking for a moment*). I'm taking a little mental snapshot of you, something to store away in my mind. Because, you see . . . I'm seeing you for the last time.

(*For the space of about five seconds, none of them speak. Then they all exclaim together:*)

Gertie		You're *what*?
Edith	(*simultaneously*).	Mother, what do you mean?
Alice		But, Mother——

Mrs. Treetops. I'm going away in a day or two —and what's more, I'm not coming back.

Edith (*instantly*). Now, Mother, please—you're not to do anything in a hurry!

ALICE (*her words following immediately upon* EDITH'S). No—now listen, Mother—you come and talk to Henry—Henry will arrange things for you.

MRS. TREETOPS. Henry's too late. They're arranged. I'm taking a nice little flat in London—in Kensington.

EDITH
ALICE }(*simultaneously*). *Kensington?*
GERTIE

MRS. TREETOPS. And what's wrong with Kensington? It's a very respectable place. Queen Victoria was born there.

EDITH (*wildly*). But London—it'll kill you—it'll kill you in a year!

MRS. TREETOPS (*calmly*). Let it. I'll have crammed more into that year than you in your whole life. And another thing——

GERTIE. Now, Mother, *do* listen to *reason*!

MRS. TREETOPS (*slightly louder*). And another thing I'd like to mention in passing: I've made my will.

(*There is a little involuntary movement of hand or head from each of the three.*)

Not one of you gets a penny.

(ALICE *and* GERTIE *stiffen.* EDITH *makes a convulsive movement, as though about to spring to her feet, then restrains the impulse.*)

ALICE. I'm sure . . . I'm not thinking of myself. . . .

MRS. TREETOPS. Oh, no, you're thinking of those horrid chicks. (*Firmly.*) Not one penny. I can't bear the sight of them. I never thought to see a baby with shifty eyes, Alice, but your baby has got 'em, all right.

ALICE. Oh, *Mother!*—oh, what a *dreadful* thing to say! I've got two wonderful children! Everybody says so! (*Once more the handkerchief is whisked from her handbag and brought into play.*)

Mrs. Treetops. All right, Alice, all right. I know what's on your mind.

Edith (*controlling herself with an effort*). Mother—I ask you—come back to the Vicarage with me—let Arthur talk to you—please——

Mrs. Treetops. Arthur ? Yes, I suppose he'd see me as a promising customer now—try to sell me Heaven as though it were a vacuum-cleaner. I've heard him at it.

Gertie. Oh, Mother !

Mrs. Treetops. I know your idea of Heaven, too, Gertie—a field the size of Salisbury Plain, with a lot of great whacking angels tearing about with golden hockey-sticks ! (*A short laugh.*)

(Gertie *makes as though to rise indignantly, but :*)

Edith (*hastily—a restraining hand on* Gertie's *knee*). Gertie, *please* ! Mother doesn't mean one-half she's saying. (*To* Mrs. Treetops—*cajolingly.*) Now, Mother, we're going to forget all this, London and everything. This wonderful thing that's happened has unbalanced you—it would anybody—but in a few days' time, you'll be able to think more clearly, and we'll have another little talk . . . make some really sensible plans for you.

Mrs. Treetops. Not if I know it ! (*She rises, and there is about her an air of finality, like one who, having read to the end of a book, closes it for ever.*) It's no use. You can talk till you're black in the face. My mind's made up.

Edith. But—we can't let you go off like this—on your own—it simply isn't to be thought of!

Mrs. Treetops (*with just a hint of harshness in her voice*). You were finding it easy enough to think of just now. All you wanted then was to get me as far away as possible ! I was to be dumped in a Home for old women and forgotten, wasn't I ?—like an old dog that's grown to be a bit of nuisance ! Tie a brick round its neck and drop it into the canal ! (*She has started to cross in front of them towards down* L.)

GERTIE (*explosively*). Mother!—You've no *right* to say such things!

ALICE (*still sniffing and dabbing at her eyes*). She couldn't, either, if she'd ever really loved us! But she never has! Not even when we were children!

MRS. TREETOPS (*down* L.—*very deliberately*). I should think not! You were three of the most unlovable children you'd meet in a day's march—and as women, frankly, I think you're detestable!

EDITH (*springing to her feet—her fists clenched*). *Mother!*

MRS. TREETOPS (*ignoring the interruption—relentlessly*). Detestable! Cold, mean, snobbish and joyless, with tiny shrivelled-up hearts ticking away inside you, and—and lemon-juice in your veins!

(EDITH *takes a step towards her.*)

Sit down, Edith!

(*It is clear that nothing is going to stop her now.* EDITH *sits abruptly.*)

For years now you've been ashamed of me! (*As they open their mouths to protest—flinging out one hand towards them.*) Don't dare to deny it!—Ashamed! You've made positions for yourselves in the town! Three big frogs in a dull little pond! You're somebodies now! You fancy yourselves! And I don't fit in! I'm just a shade common, and I let you down! I go into public-houses and drink a glass of sherry. I hum little songs to myself as I walk along the street! I laugh too often and too loudly! In fact, I'm all the things that you thank God you're not!

ALICE. Oh—Mother—oh, how *can* you?

MRS. TREETOPS. So I must be kept well in the background, and only asked to your homes when you're quite, quite sure that none of your fine friends will be calling. Oh, I'm the family skeleton, all right! I know!

GERTIE (*heatedly*). It's all very well for you to

say these things now! Where'd you have been all these years if it hadn't been for us? (*She rises.*) You've been thankful enough to live on our charity!

MRS. TREETOPS (*more quietly*). Charity! Yes! It ought to be a beautiful word. Charity. But somehow it isn't.

(*As* GERTIE *turns impatiently and goes a little way up* L.—*in a different tone.*)

I'm glad it's only money I owe you, and not affection, because it means that I can pay you back. I'll work it out to the penny this evening and send you cheques.

EDITH (*rising—a step or two forward*). No, Mother, you're not to! (*Pulling herself together for a last effort.*) Now listen: we shall come and see you again to-morrow, and talk to you. Arthur will come, too.

ALICE (*rising—stuffing her handkerchief back into her bag*). Yes—yes, and I'll bring Henry. That's an idea!

(GERTIE *moves behind the settee, to by the* R. *end of it.*)

MRS. TREETOPS (*bluntly*). And an idea's all it ever will be!—From now on, my life's my own pie, and you can just keep your ladylike fingers out of it! By this time next week, Katie and I will be in London, and——

EDITH (*shrilly—as though this is indeed the last straw*). Katie? You mean—you're taking that vulgar Boxer woman with you? Good *heavens*! What *next*?

MRS. TREETOPS (*calmly*). And why not? We understand one another, Katie and I—yes, we understand one another.

EDITH (*fuming*). I'd be ashamed to admit it! A creature like that! The scum of the earth!

ALICE (*going to beside* EDITH—R. *of her*). But she's dreadful! You've only got to look at her!

MRS. TREETOPS (*still calmly*). I doubt if you'd look

much better, Alice, if you'd spent as many years as she has—in prison.

EDITH. *Prison? Prison*, did you say?

MRS. TREETOPS. Yes! Prison!—For having the courage to answer a brute of a husband in the only language he understood—a smack over the head with a meat-axe.

ALICE (*with a horrified gasp*). You don't mean—she—murdered her husband? Oh, no!

MRS. TREETOPS (*after a quick nod*). At first, they were for hanging Katie Boxer . . . but they changed their minds and kept her in prison instead . . . and then one day—a first of April, it was—long, long after—they let her go.

EDITH (*her voice rising*). And you—you tolerate a degraded character like that about you?—It's worse even than I thought!—It's terrible!

GERTIE (*joining her sisters*—R. *of* ALICE). A murderess? A—a gaol-bird?—Well, what else is she?

ALICE. Oh, *Mother*!

EDITH. How you can *bear* to have her in the house! How you *can*!

MRS. TREETOPS (*in a quite level tone*). You wouldn't have her in your house, would you, Edith?

EDITH (*drawing herself up*). I? I should think not, indeed! Whatever you may lack, *we've* got our pride, you know.

(*A tiny pause. Then:*)

MRS. TREETOPS (*in the same level tone—looking at her very steadily*). Yes, you've got your pride, all right. (*As though suddenly making up her mind.*) And I'm now going to do to that pride, what Katie Boxer did to her husband! (*A shade louder.*) I'm going to hit it over the head—hard!

GERTIE. What d'you mean?

MRS. TREETOPS. And I warn you: it's going to hurt! It's going to give you three a pain you'll never get rid of as long as you live!

EDITH (*sharply—with the sharpness of one who, hearing a noise in the dark, calls out " What's that ? "*). What are you talking about ?—Eh ?

(*The positions now are : the three sisters, EDITH, ALICE and GERTIE, in that order, are standing slightly to* L. *of the* L. *end of the settee. They must not be in a straight line :* EDITH *should be a little apart from them, and a pace more forward.* MRS. TREETOPS *is facing them, midway between them and the door.*)

MRS. TREETOPS (*slowly, so that every word " tells "*). When Katie Boxer went to prison, I did what I thought was a great and glorious thing. . . . I took her three children . . . reared them . . . brought them up as my own. . . . Their names were Edith, Alice and Gertie.

(*In the stricken silence that follows, the first reaction of the three is that they have not heard aright ; the second is that this is " another of Mother's so-called jokes," and in even worse than usual taste ; the third, the inevitable, relentless third, is the sudden, fear-clutching, nightmare doubt. . . . These reactions follow one another very swiftly, so that the silence lasts no more than a few seconds. Then :*)

EDITH (*in an unnaturally loud voice*). Mother ! D'you know what you're saying ?

(MRS. TREETOPS *does not speak.*)

Mother, d'you hear ?—What you said just now— you're to tell us at once—it isn't true ! (*Her voice suddenly snaps off.*)

(MRS. TREETOPS' *only answer is to go to the door and fling it open.*)

MRS. TREETOPS (*calling*). Katie ! Katie ! Come here ! I want you !

MRS. BOXER'S VOICE (*from the kitchen*). Righto, Missis !

MRS. TREETOPS (*to the three—in an almost conversational tone*). You may like to have your birth certificates. I'll post them along with the cheques.

ALICE (*suddenly*). No, no! No! (*Her voice, like* EDITH'S, *seems to snap off.*)

MRS. TREETOPS. It's no trouble.

(*As* MRS. BOXER *appears in the doorway.*)

Ah, Katie.

(MRS. BOXER *has removed her hat, and in one hand she is carrying a coil of thin rope.*)

MRS. BOXER. I were just fetching the clothes-line in when you called. (*Then, sensing the atmosphere.*) What's up, Missis?

MRS. TREETOPS (*going to her—quietly*). I've told them.

MRS. BOXER (*startled—obviously very shaken—advancing about two steps into the room*). Oh, Missis! —Oh, Missis—you never 'ave—oh, you shouldn't 'ave——

MRS. TREETOPS (*touching her lightly on the shoulder*). It was best, Katie.

(*And without another glance towards the three, she goes out. There is a short, petrified silence. The sisters have drawn a little closer together at* MRS. BOXER'S *entrance, but now there is no movement whatever. They stare at her with a sort of dumb and horrified fascination. And then, from the outside world, there drifts into the room the sound of a church clock chiming the two quarter chimes sounding the half-hour, and:*)

MRS. BOXER (*looking the very picture of embarrassment—then, making an effort to pull herself together—forcing a sheepish, nervous grin, and the only words that her whirling thoughts can muster*). Well, girls . . . ?

The notes of the church clock seem still to hang upon the air as :

The CURTAIN *falls.*

www.ingramcontent.com/pod-product-compliance
Lightning Source LLC
Chambersburg PA
CBHW051413290426
44108CB00015B/2269